I ♥ ME
COLORING BOOK
A BOOK OF POSITIVE AFFIRMATIONS

Illustrated by
Sherrell Satterthwaite

I AM WORTHY OF RESPECT

I AM NOT
OTHER
PEOPLE'S
OPINIONS
OF ME

I GIVE MYSELF SPACE AND TIME TO HEAL

I AM WORTHY OF LOVE

I ATTRACT LOVING RELATIONSHIPS INTO MY LIFE.

I create
I want

the life
to live

PEACE, LOVE
AND POSSIBILITIES
BREAK OUT
EVERYWHERE
I GO

I rel

dis-e

my body

health, hap

and love

ease all
ase from
and welcome
piness, wealth
into my life

I AM ALLOWED TO SAY NO

IN ALL
THINGS
I AM
GRATEFUL

I AM HERE
FOR A DIVINE
PURPOSE

I AM MY SISTER'S KEEPER. WE LOVE, INSPIRE AND UPLIFT ONE ANOTHER

CARING FOR MY HAIR IS AN AFFIRMATION OF LOVE OF SELF

Made in the USA
Middletown, DE
25 September 2022

11136633R00031